SCHUBERT MASTERPIECES
for Solo Piano
19 Works

FRANZ SCHUBERT

DOVER PUBLICATIONS, INC.
Mineola, New York

Bibliographical Note

This Dover edition, first published in 2002, is a new compilation of works originally published in the Schubert Complete Works Edition by Breitkopf & Härtel, Leipzig, in 1888–9, edited by Julius Epstein.

International Standard Book Number: 0-486-42200-3

Manufactured in the United States of America
Dover Publications, Inc., 31 East 2nd Street, Mineola, N.Y. 11501

CONTENTS

SCHUBERT
MASTERPIECES
for Solo Piano

Scherzo in B-flat major

No. 1 of *Two Scherzi*, D593 (November 1817)

Scherzo da Capo.

Sonata in A major

D664/Op. posth. 120 (July 1819)

Andante.

Allegro.

14   Sonata in A

"Wanderer" Fantasy

Fantasy in C: D760/Op. 15 (November 1822)

[The 2nd movement, p. 26, is based on Schubert's song "Der Wanderer," D493.]

Allegro con fuoco ma non troppo.

Adagio.

6 Moments Musicaux

D780/Op. 94 (1823–8)

[No. 3 was published separately as "Air russe," 1823; No. 6, as "Plaintes d'un Troubadour," 1824]

3. Allegro moderato.

Allegro vivace.

5.

Allegretto.

6.

11 Ecossaises

D781 (January 1823)

No 6.

No 7.

No 8.

№ 9.

№ 10.

№ 11.

12 Ländler

12 Deutsche Tänze: D790/Op. 171 (May 1823)

No 4.

No 5.

No 6.

No 7.

col Pedale

4 Impromptus

From Opp. 90 & 142

Impromptu in E-flat major

D899/Op. 90 no. 2 (1827?)

Impromptu in G-flat major

D899/Op. 90 no. 3 (1827?)

Impromptu in B-flat major

D935/Op. 142 no. 3 (December 1827)

VAR. IV.

Impromptu in F minor

D935/Op. 142 no. 4 (December 1827)

Allegro scherzando.

In remembrance of my dear friend [Ferdinand] Walcher

Allegretto in C minor

D915 (April 1827)

102 Allegretto

3 Piano Pieces

D946 (*ca.* May 1828)

[Originally planned as four Impromptus—in the manner of Opp. 90 and 142—these pieces were published posthumously under the title *Drei Klavierstucke*, edited anonymously by Johannes Brahms.]

1.

2.

3.

Allegro.